MW00897424

THIS COLORING BOOK
BELONGS TO:

_____

- - - - - - - - - - - - - - - -

- - - - - - - - - - - - - - - -

_____

2022 - ALL RIGHTS RESERVED

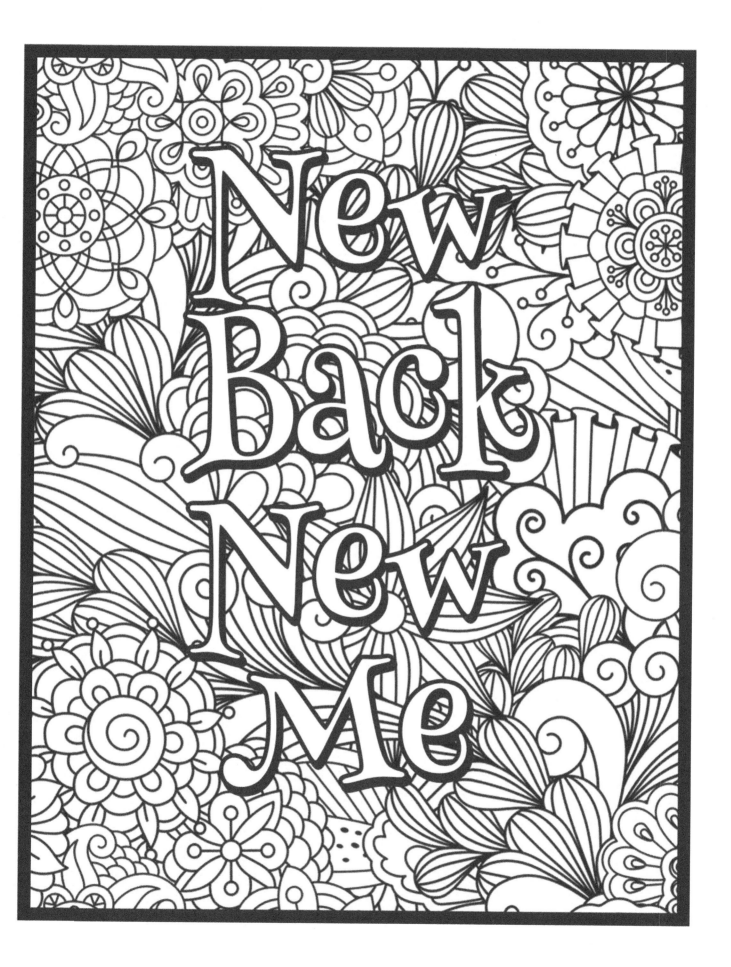

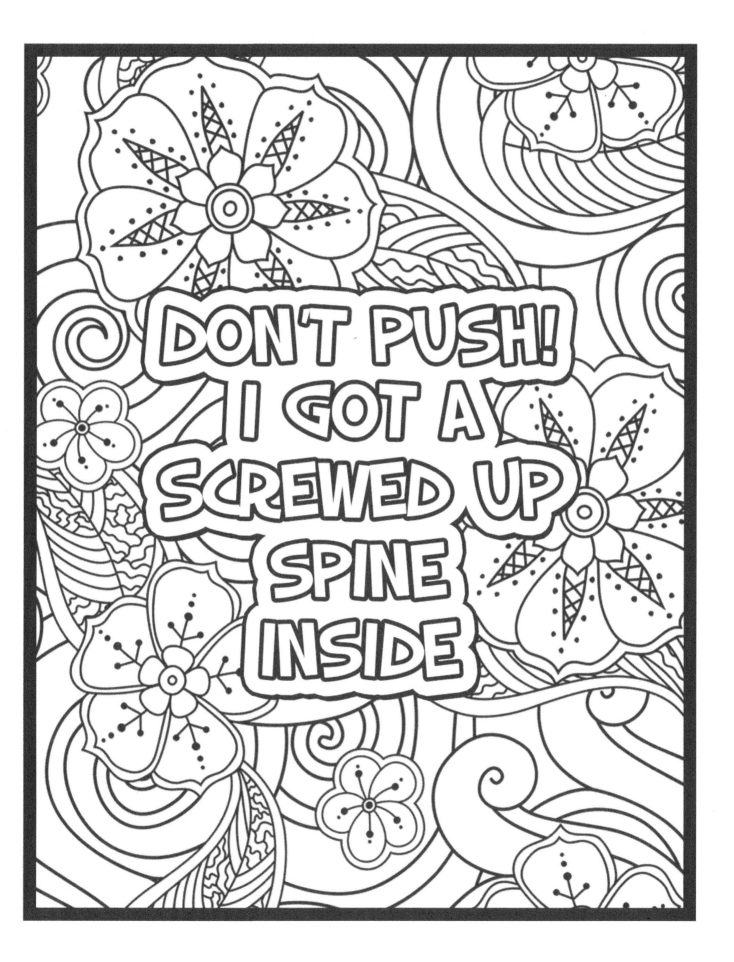

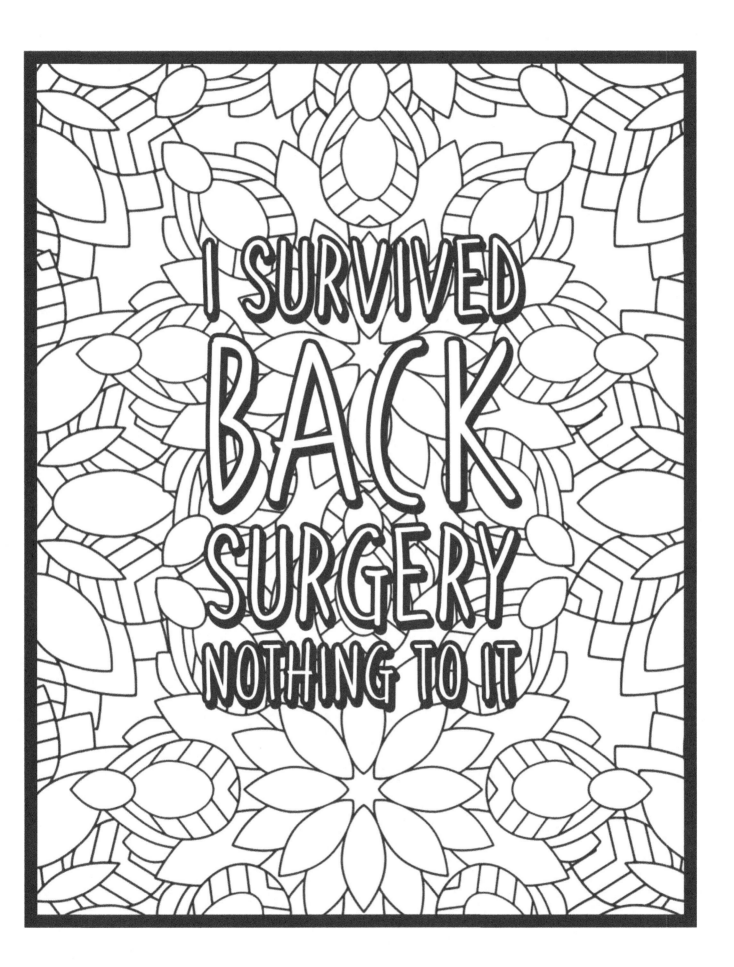

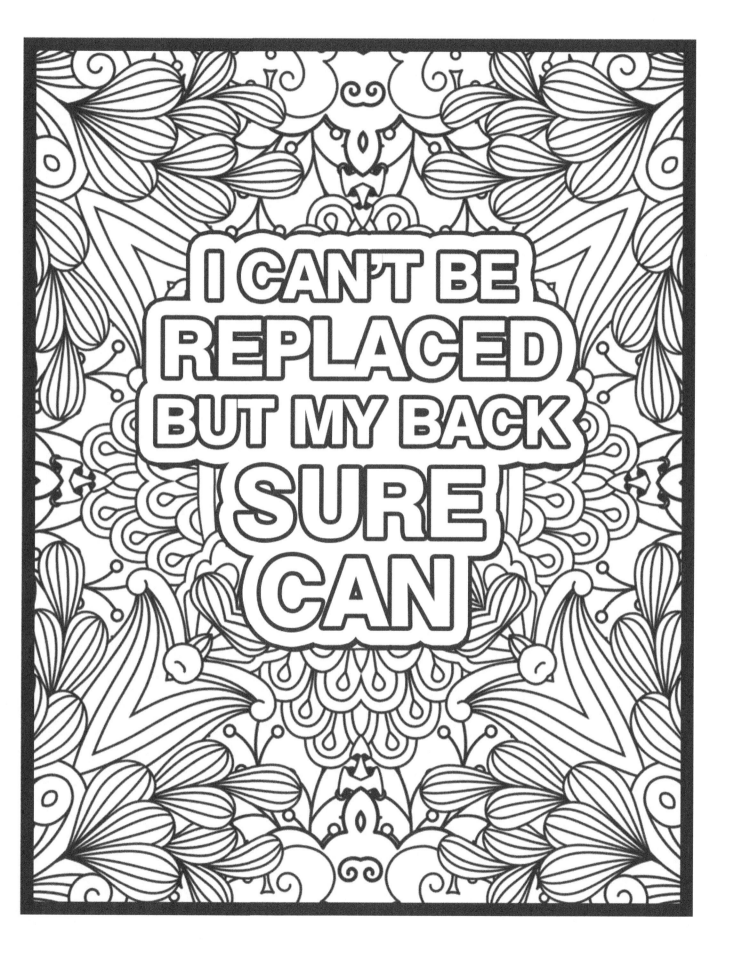

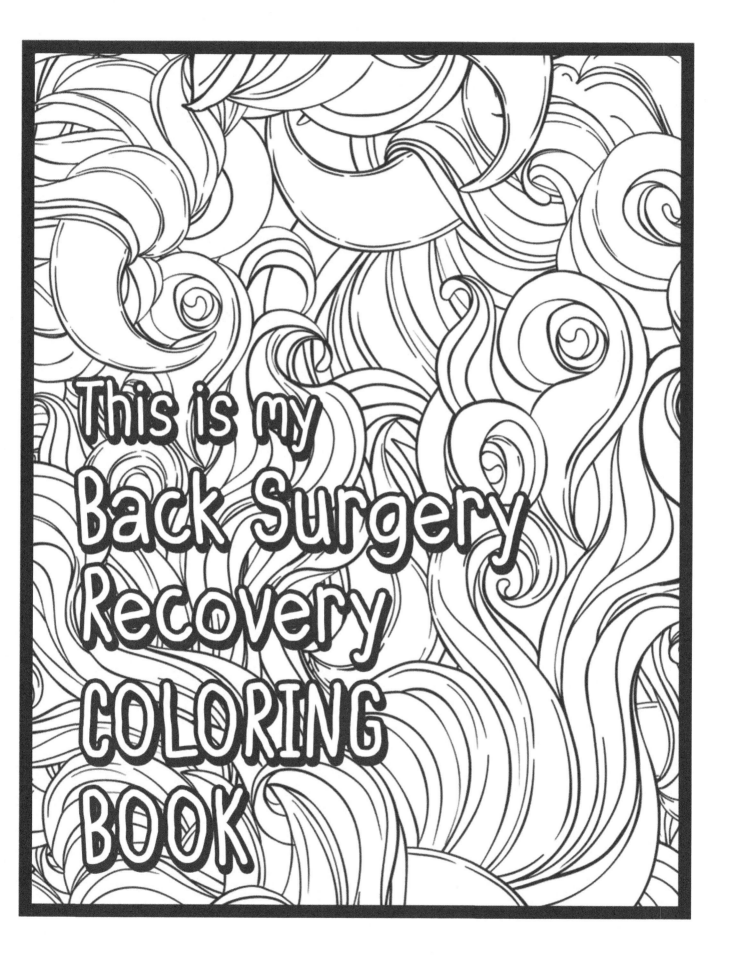

This is my
Back Surgery
Recovery
COLORING
BOOK

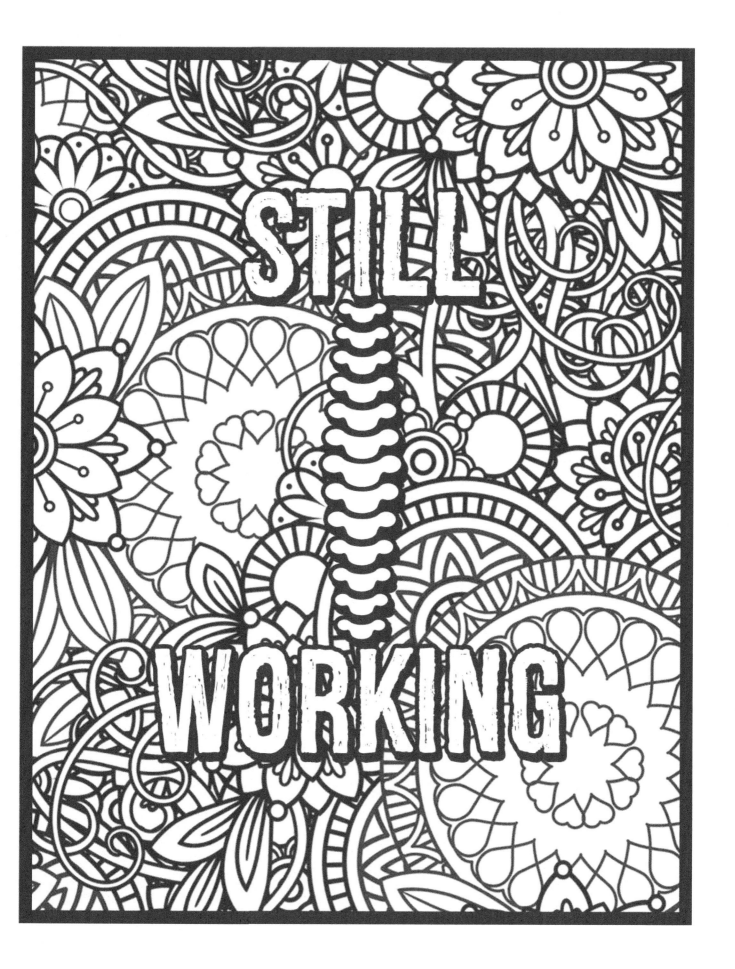

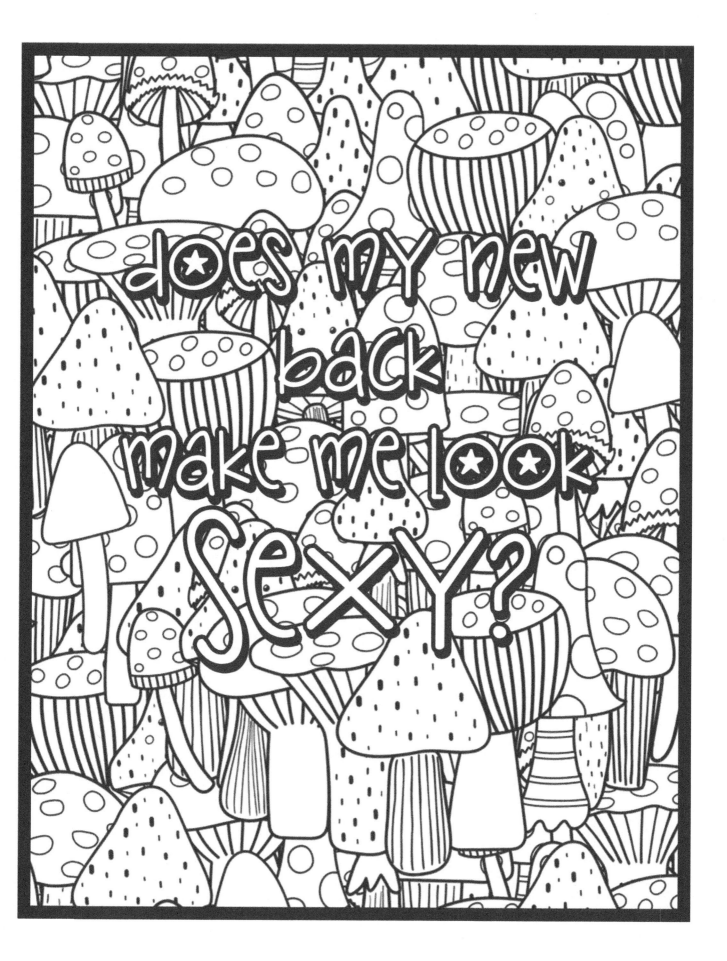

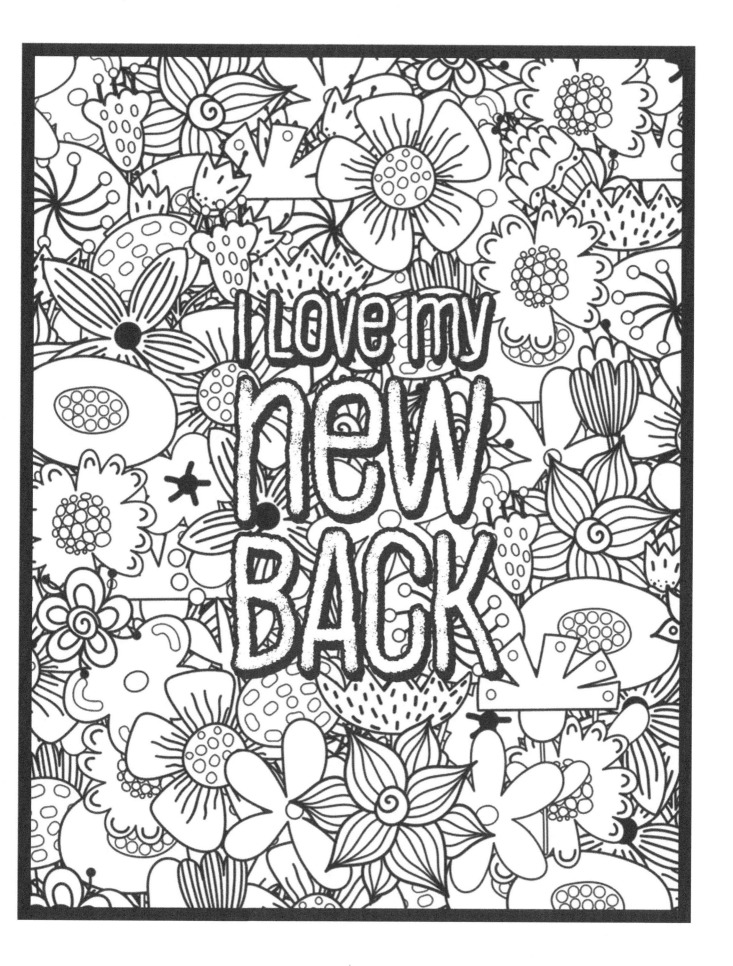

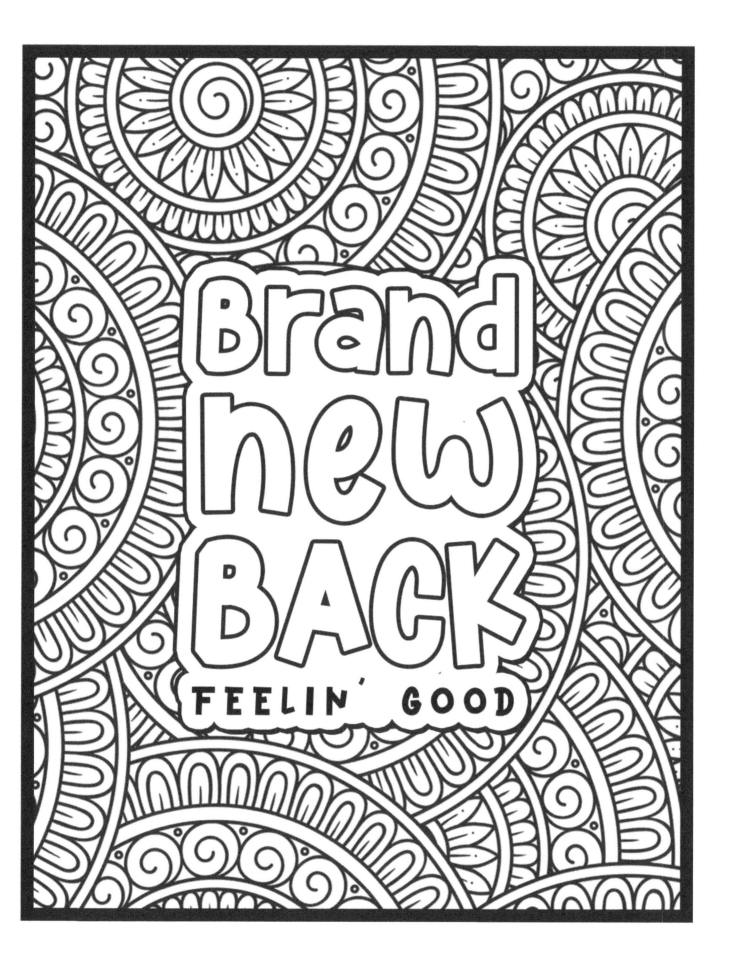

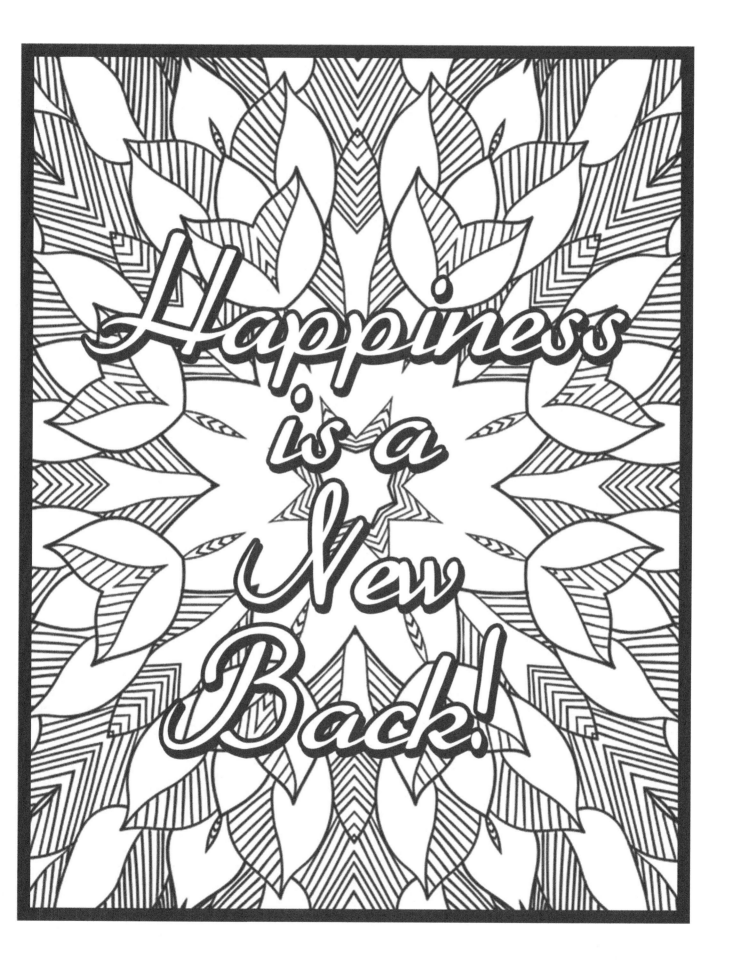

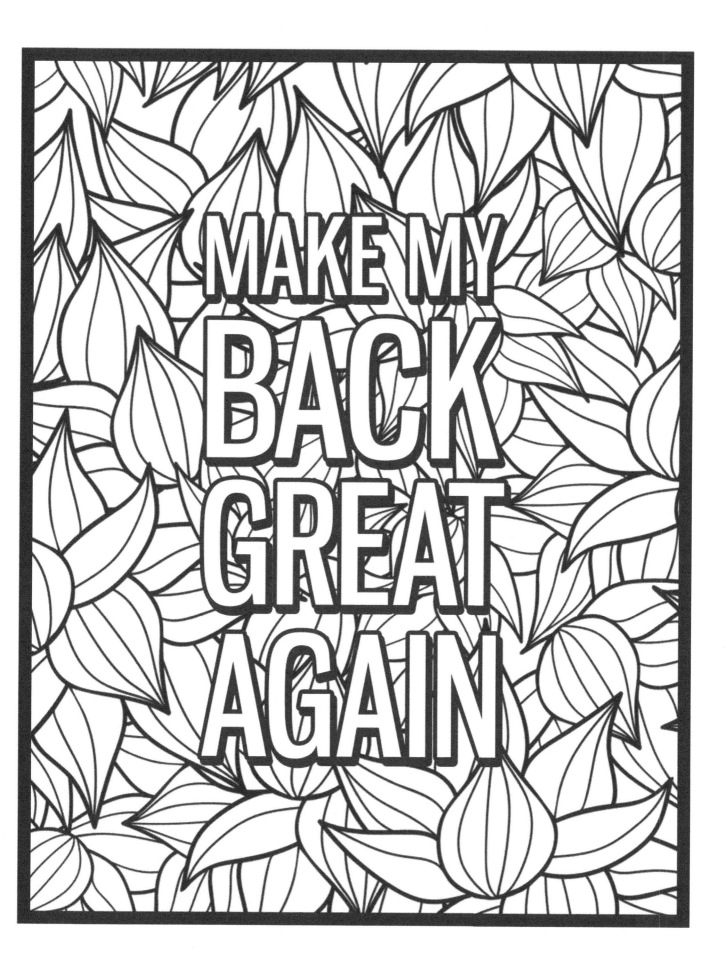

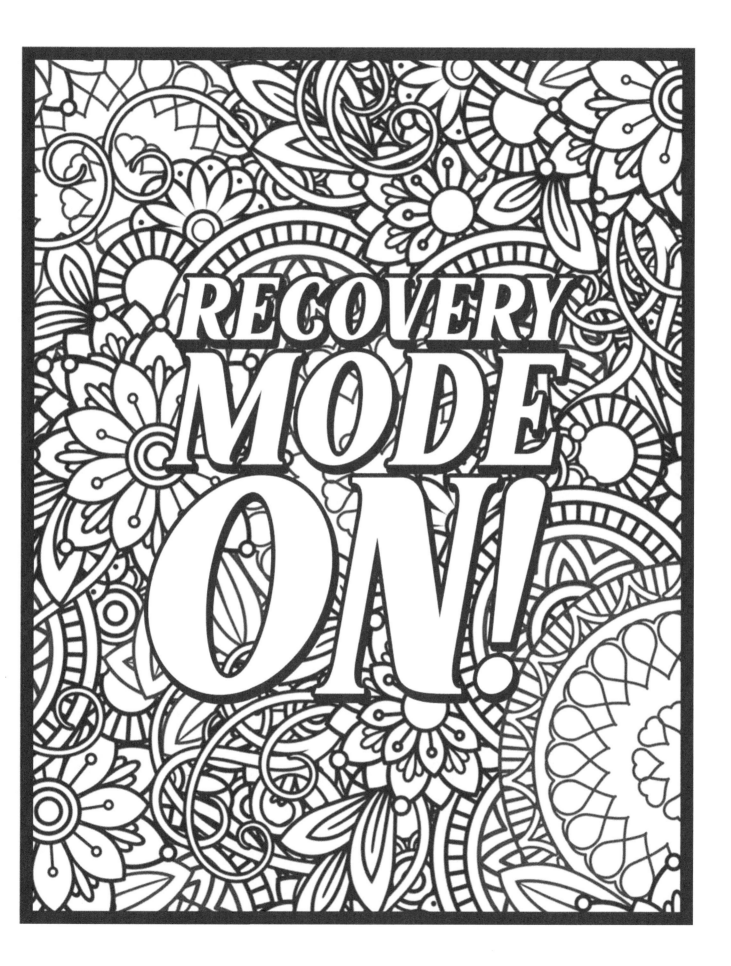

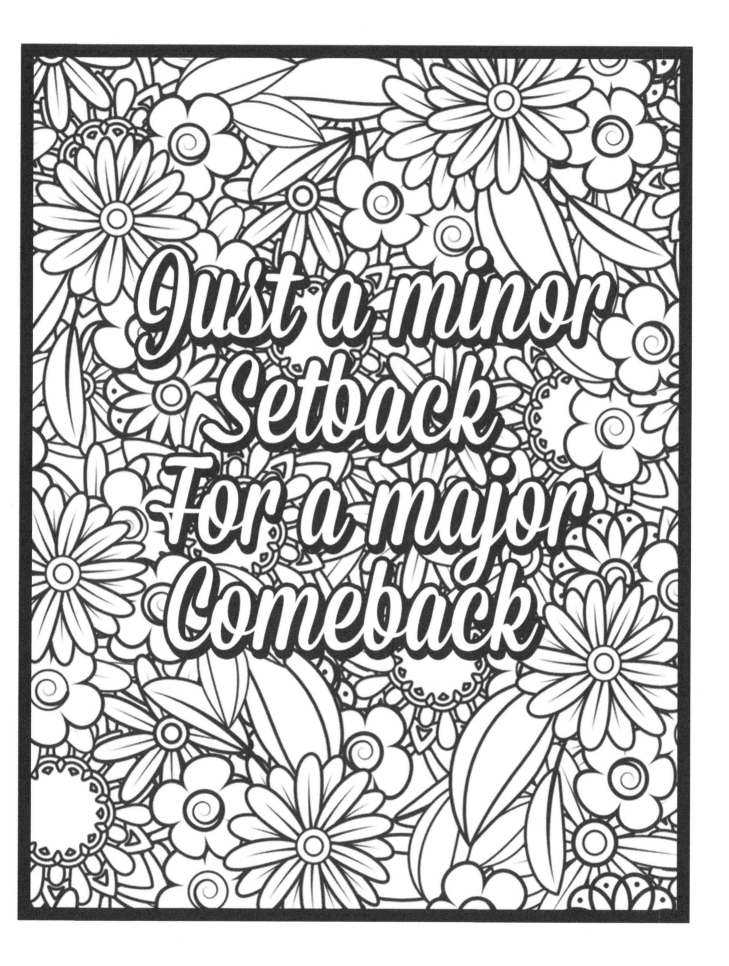

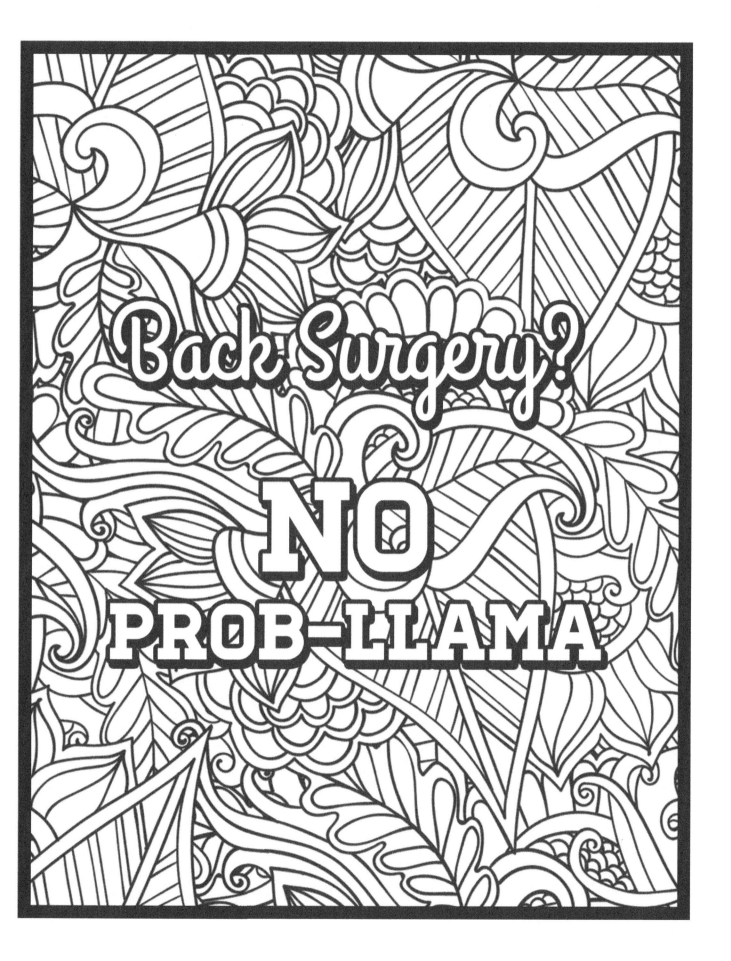

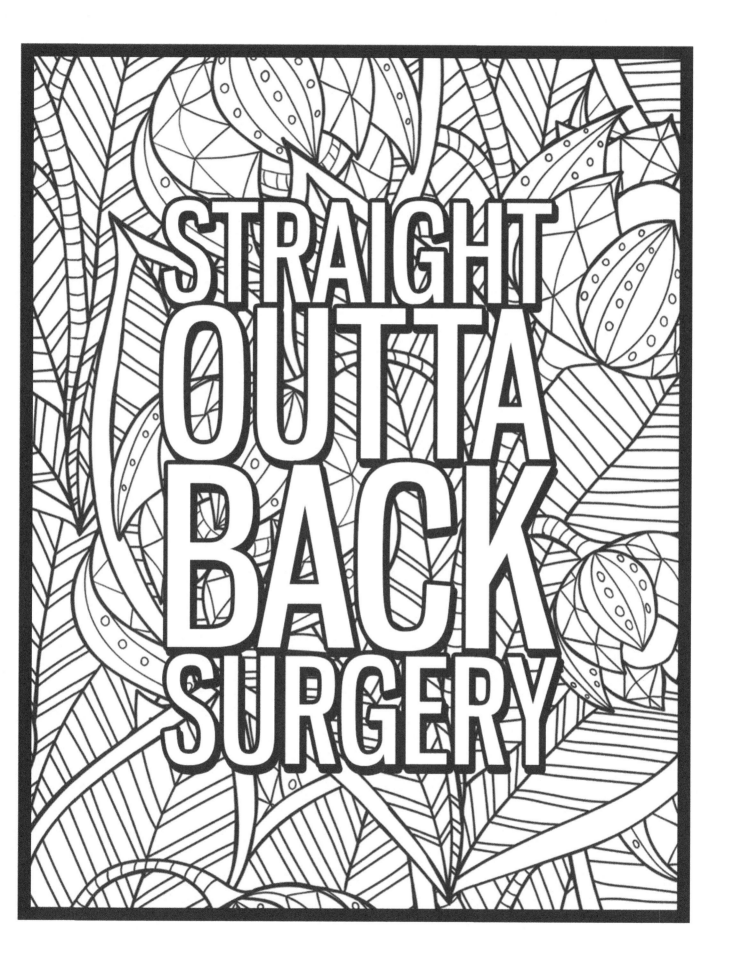

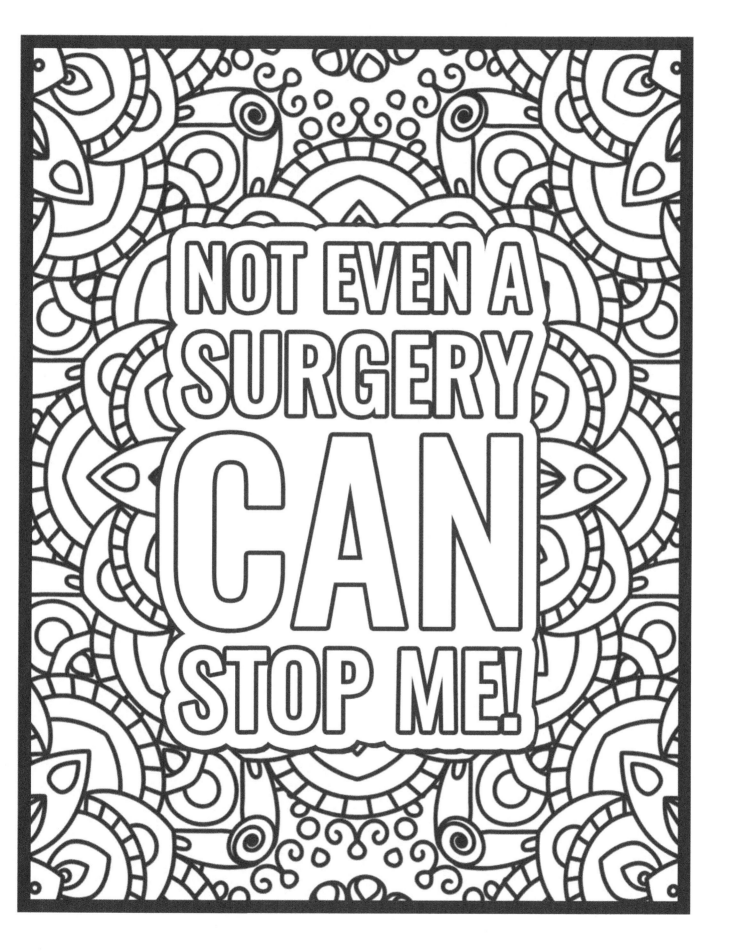

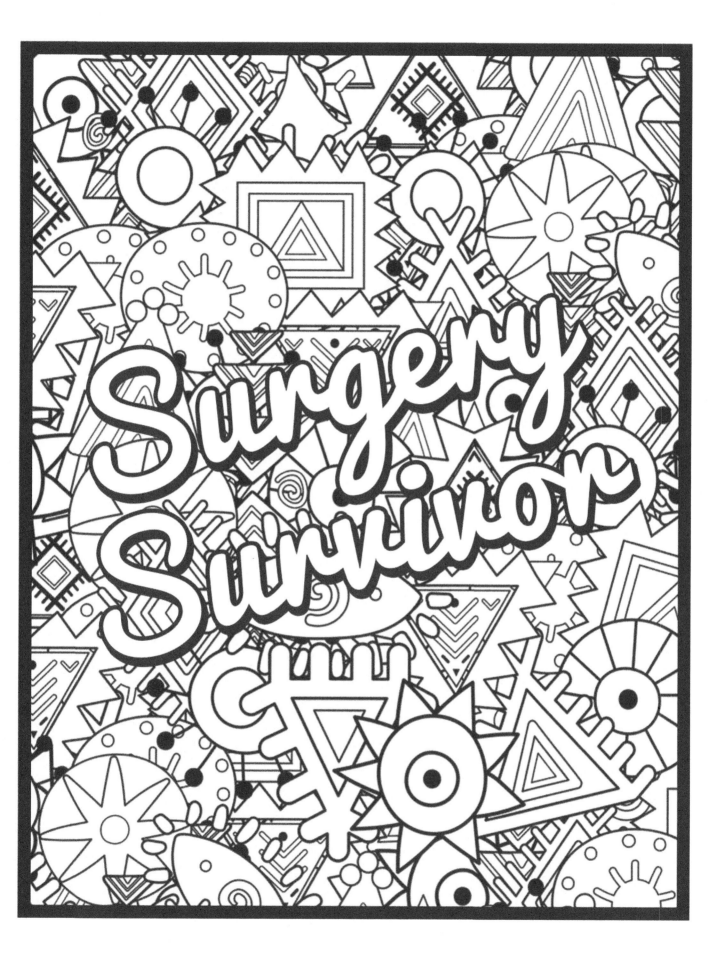

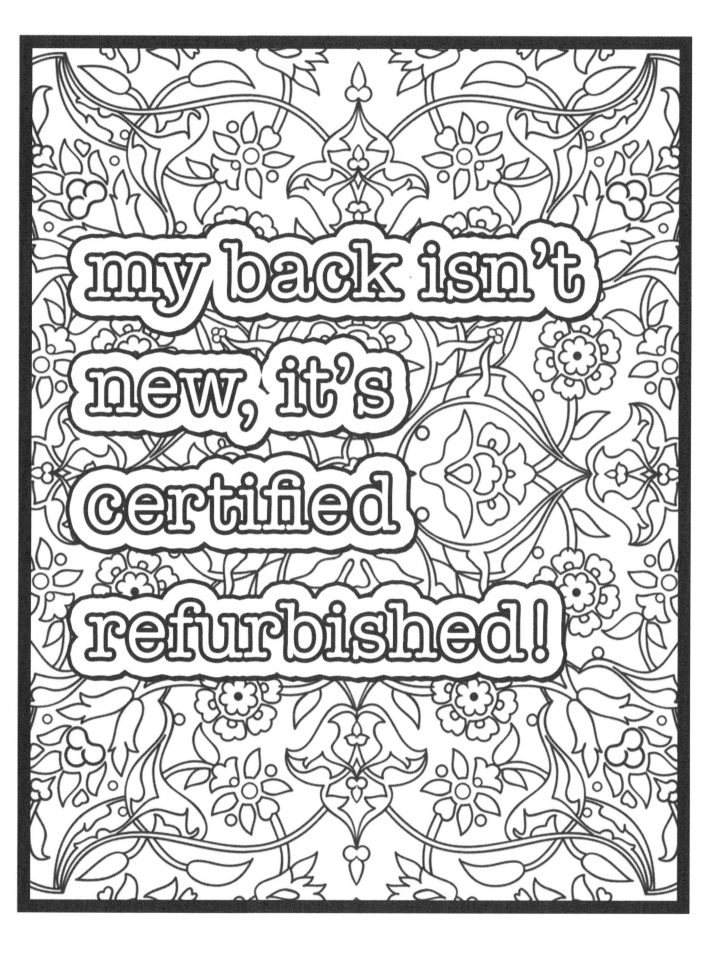

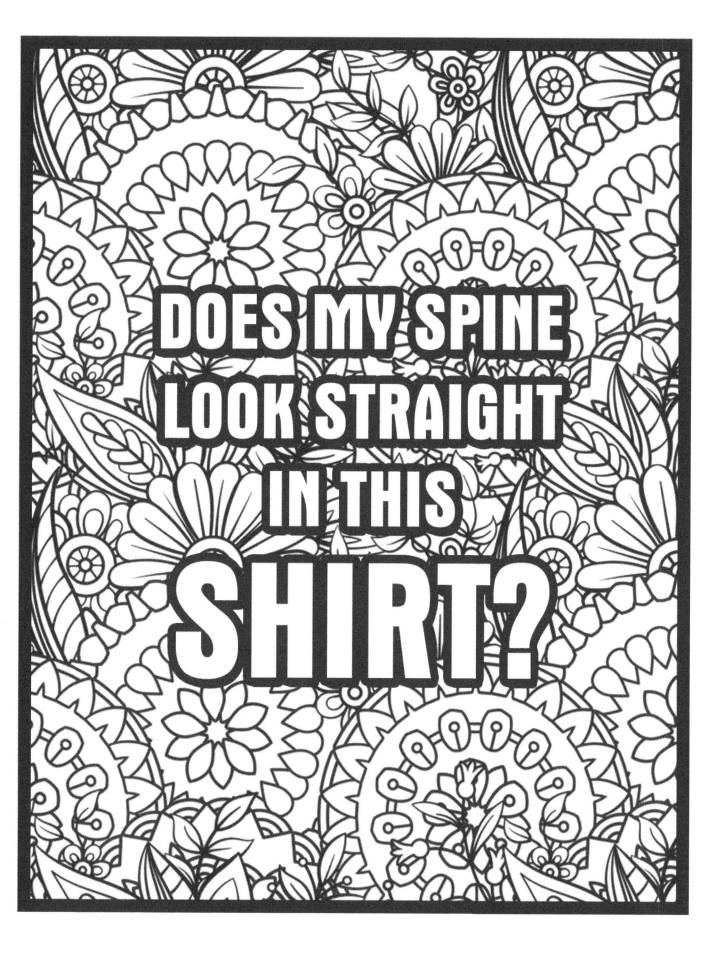

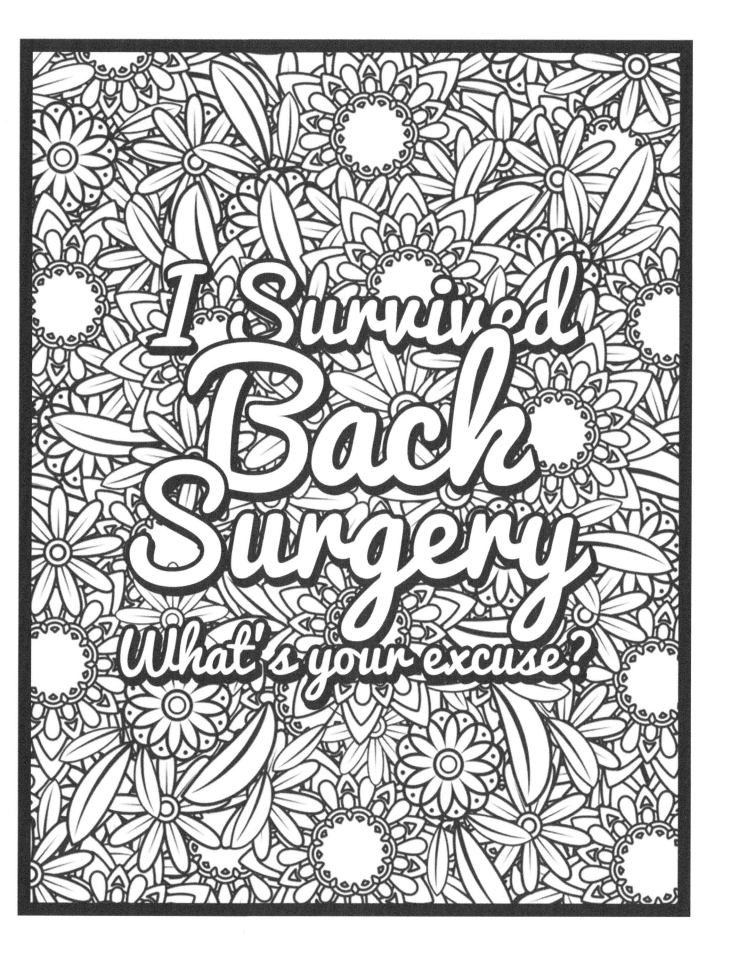

Made in the USA
Las Vegas, NV
09 May 2024

89733857R00024